TRAVEL BUG GOES TO NEW YORK CITY

WRITTEN BY
BOBBY BASIL

3 FREE BOOKS!

I'm Travel Bug, and I love to travel!

I traveled very far
from my
home planet . . .

All the way to Earth!

I want to see and learn EVERYTHING about your planet!

On Earth,
I travel on a plane.

Planes can fly
all around
the world.

Today I am flying to New York City!

That's a city in the United States of America.

New York City is in the state of New York.

What do you think the state looks like?

New York City is in the southeast corner of the state.

New York City

The city is on the east coast of the United States.

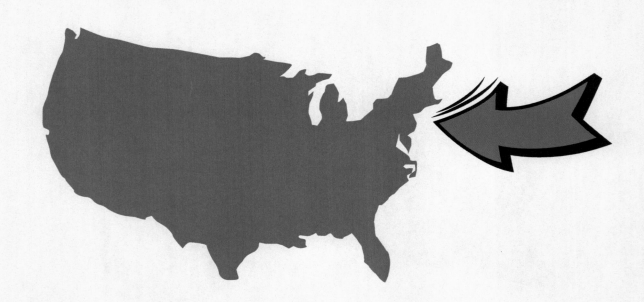

That means it's right next to the ocean!

In 1664, the city was named after the Duke of York.

He would become King James II of England.

The city is the most populous in the U.S.

Over 8.6 million people live there!

The people who live in NYC come from very different backgrounds.

In the 1800s, many Irish and German immigrants sailed to New York to escape bad things in Europe.

Starting in 1892, immigrants landed at Ellis Island.

The Statue of Liberty welcomed them to America.

Immigrants still move to New York City.

Now they arrive from all over the world.

Over 3 million people living there were born outside The United States.

They speak 800 languages in the city!

It's exciting having different backgrounds.

People can share things and learn about each other.

My favorite place in New York City is Broadway.

You can watch actors sing and dance in musicals!

New York City has delicious food from all over the world.

They have tasty pizza!

A nickname for New York City is The Big Apple.

I'm getting hungry talking about food!

I had a lot of fun in New York City.

I can't wait to travel with you again!

PLEASE
LEAVE A REVIEW
ON AMAZON!

Your review will
help other readers
discover my books.
Thank you!

Made in the USA
Las Vegas, NV
03 December 2023

82035387R00017